Disney Movie Hits

SONG TITLE	PAGE NUMBER	TRACK WITH MELODY CUE	TRACK ACCOMPANIMENT ONLY
Belle	2	1	13
A Whole New World	4	2	14
Prince Ali	6	3	15
God Help the Outcasts	8	4	16
Hakuna Matata	9	5	17
Beauty and the Beast	10	6	18
Cruella De Vil	12	7	19
When She Loved Me	14	8	20
Kiss the Girl	15	9	21
If I Didn't Have You	16	10	22
Go the Distance	18	11	23
Circle of Life	19	12	24
"A" Tuning Notes			25

ISBN 0-634-00101-9

Walt Disney Music Company
Wonderland Music Company, Inc.

DISTRIBUTED BY

Hal Leonard Corporation

7777 W. BLUEMOUND RD. P.O. BOX 13819 MILWAUKEE, WI 53213

Disney characters and artwork © Disney Enterprises, Inc.

These arrangements and recordings are intended for private home use only.
They may not be used in connection with any performance that includes the use of costumes,
choreography or other elements that evoke the story or characters of this musical work.

For all works contained herein:
Unauthorized copying, arranging, adapting, recording or public performance is an infringement of copyright.
Infringers are liable under the law.

Visit Hal Leonard Online at
www.halleonard.com

BELLE

From Walt Disney's BEAUTY AND THE BEAST

CD
1: With melody cue
13: Accompaniment only

Lyrics by HOWARD ASHMAN
Music by ALAN MENKEN

CELLO

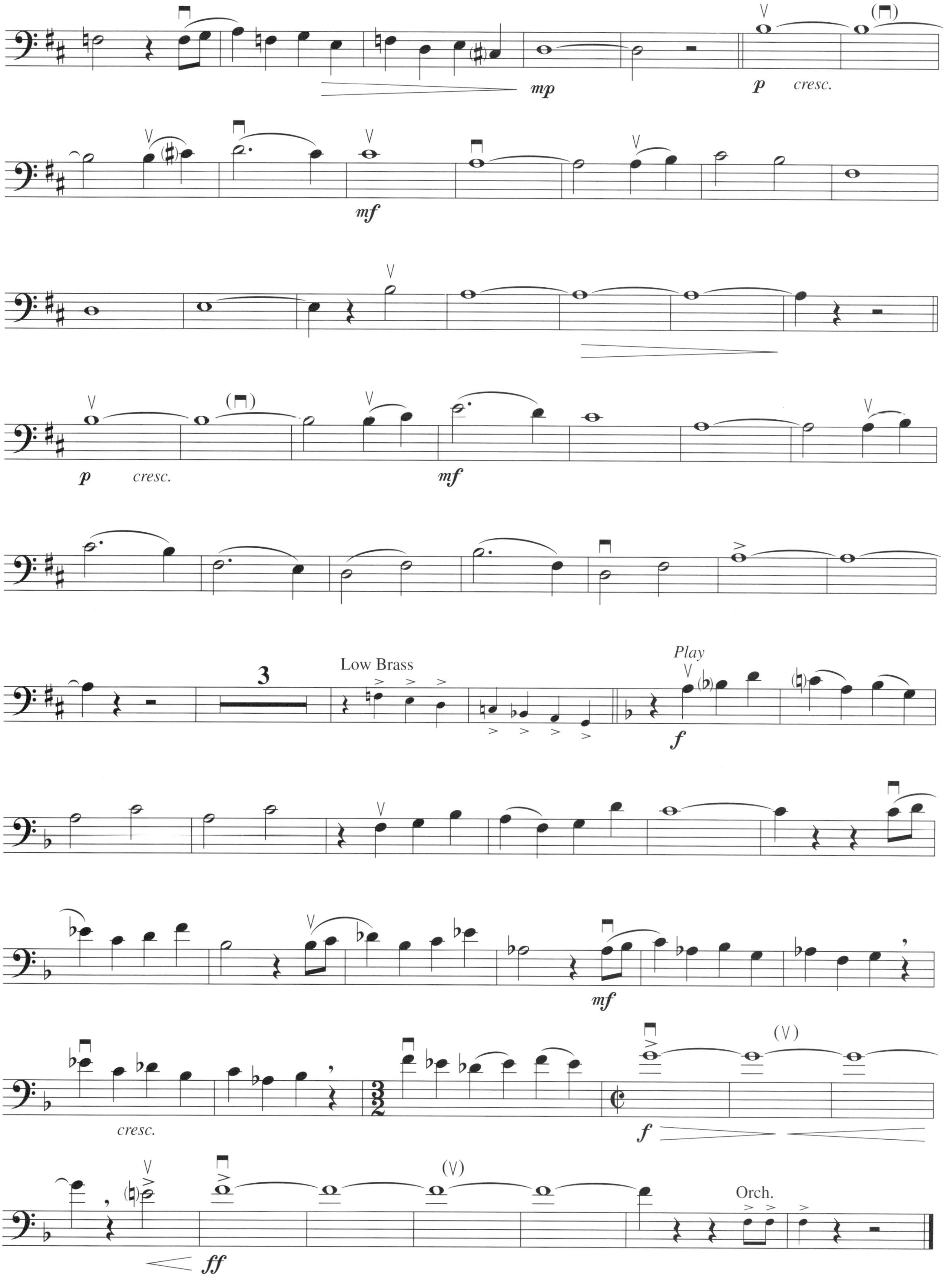
mp
p
cresc.
mf
p
cresc.
mf
3
Low Brass
Play
f
mf
cresc.
f
ff
Orch.

A WHOLE NEW WORLD

From Walt Disney's ALADDIN

Music by ALAN MANKEN
Lyrics by TIM RICE

CELLO

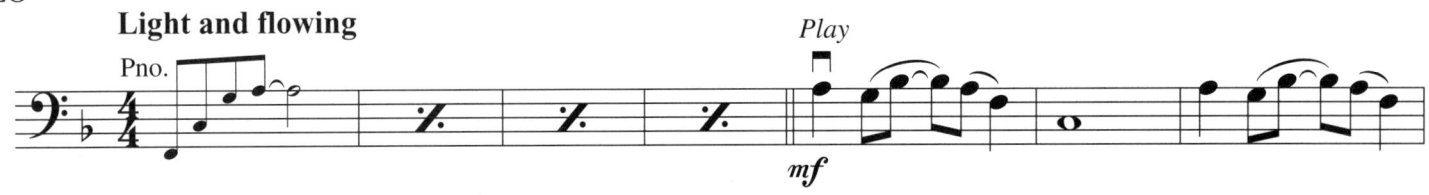

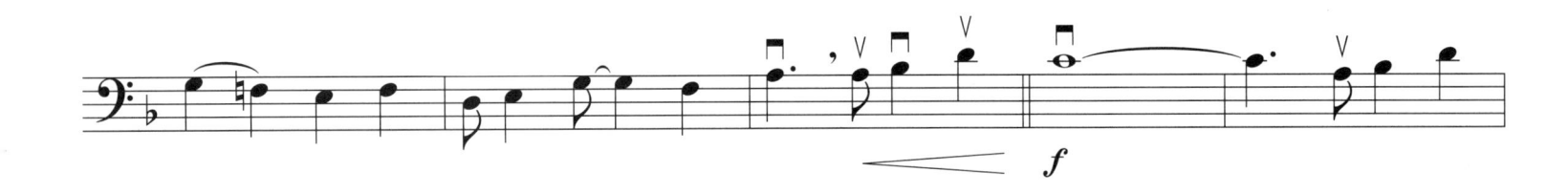

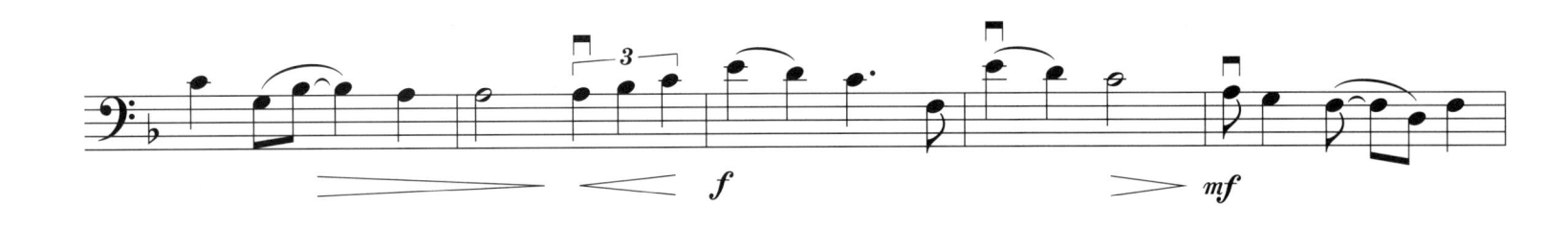

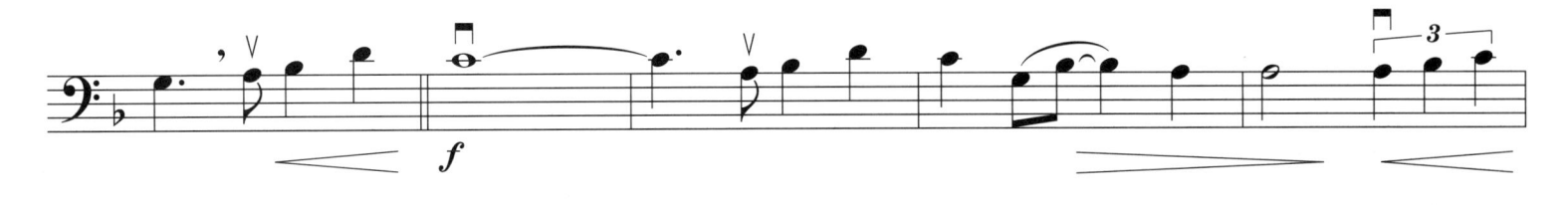

CD
- 2: With melody cue
- 14: Accompaniment only

© 1992 Wonderland Music Company, Inc. and Walt Disney Music Company
All Rights Reserved   Used by Permission

f
mf
mp
mf
3
mp
f
mf
mp
f
mf
mp
Slowing
mf
rit.
mp
Tempo I
Pno/Harp
rit.
Opt. with Orch.
p

PRINCE ALI
From Walt Disney's ALADDIN

Lyrics by HOWARD ASHMAN
Music by ALAN MENKEN

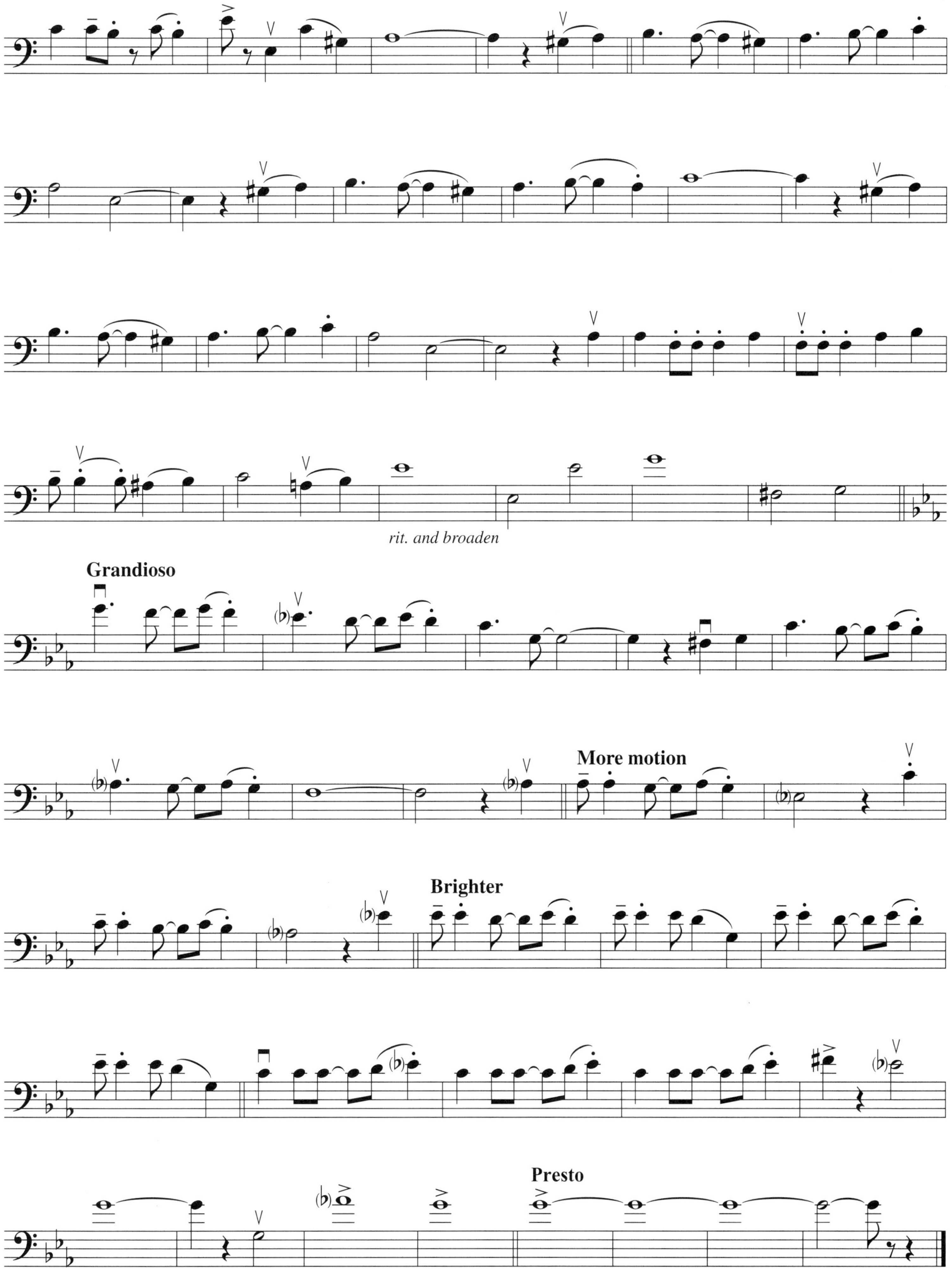
rit. and broaden
Grandioso
More motion
Brighter
Presto

GOD HELP THE OUTCASTS

From Walt Disney's THE HUNCHBACK OF NOTRE DAME

Music by ALAN MENKEN
Lyrics by STEPHEN SCHWARTZ

CELLO

© 1996 Wonderland Music Company, Inc. and Walt Disney Music Company
All Rights Reserved   Used by Permission

HAKUNA MATATA

From Walt Disney Pictures' THE LION KING

Music by ELTON JOHN
Lyrics by TIM RICE

© 1994 Wonderland Music Company, Inc.
All Rights Reserved   Used by Permission

BEAUTY AND THE BEAST
From Walt Disney's BEAUTY AND THE BEAST

Lyrics by HOWARD ASHMAN
Music by ALAN MENKEN

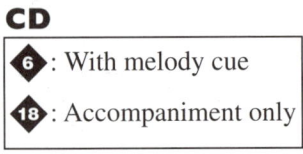

Play
mf
poco rit.
a tempo
f
mf
rit.
a tempo
2
Piano/Strings
rit.
Harp
Play
mp molto rit.

CRUELLA DE VIL

From Walt Disney's ONE HUNDRED AND ONE DALMATIANS

CD
7: With melody cue
19: Accompaniment only

Words and Music by
MEL LEVEN

CELLO

13

WHEN SHE LOVED ME

From Walt Disney Pictures' TOY STORY 2 – A Pixar Film

CD
8: With melody cue
20: Accompaniment only

Music and Lyrics by
RANDY NEWMAN

CELLO

KISS THE GIRL

From Walt Disney's THE LITTLE MERMAID

Lyrics by HOWARD ASHMAN
Music by ALAN MENKEN

IF I DIDN'T HAVE YOU

Walt Disney Pictures Presents
A Pixar Animation Studios Film MONSTERS, INC.

CD
10: With melody cue
22: Accompaniment only

Music and Lyrics by
RANDY NEWMAN

CELLO

Solo
mf
f
Slowly
mf
even 8ths
Small notes optional
Tempo I
Band
Play
f
Play
Band
mp

GO THE DISTANCE

From Walt Disney Pictures' HERCULES

Music by ALAN MENKEN
Lyrics by DAVID ZIPPEL

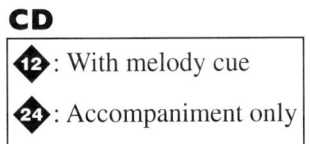

CIRCLE OF LIFE
From Walt Disney Pictures' THE LION KING

Music by ELTON JOHN
Lyrics by TIM RICE